Martha Louise Brett

Flag Days of the Twin City Public Schools

Martha Louise Brett

Flag Days of the Twin City Public Schools

ISBN/EAN: 9783337258375

Printed in Europe, USA, Canada, Australia, Japan

Cover: Foto ©Suzi / pixelio.de

More available books at **www.hansebooks.com**

*"Hurrah for our flag!
Our beautiful flag!
Our glory and also our boast,
Its colors so true,
The red, white and blue,
Have marshaled many a host."*

FLAG DAYS

—OF—

The Twin City Public Schools.

—BY—

Martha Louise Brett,

Teacher in Minneapolis Public Schools.

A. B. FARNHAM & Co.,
PRINTERS,
MINNEAPOLIS, MINN.

To my dear Mother,
who loves schools, children and teachers,
this little volume
is affectionately dedicated.

PREFACE.

Knowing, from experience, that a teacher has all she can do to attend to her daily routine of business, and that the fact of such or such a day being flag day having escaped her memory, the thought often came to me, on the arrival of such a day, that if some one would only arrange these flag days, with notes on the same, for us, who haven't the time to look the matter up properly, how relieved we would be, and how much more the scholars would be benefited by the results. Well, as that some one failed to appear, I have taken it upon myself to put my thoughts in print, hoping that the teachers and scholars may be benefited by my feeble efforts, and that honor may be done to the flag day they represent.

M. L. B.

SUGGESTIONS.

On special flag days—I say special, because all school days in St. Paul are flag days—it would be appropriate and valuable to have much of the work of the day done on the subject that date represents. For instance, the reading and spelling lessons could be obtained from poems, speeches, or from the lives of the persons, or the description of the things designated. The drawing lesson from some pose representing the subject or copying from some sketches. Geography and history can easily be obtained from each subject, and very valuable language lessons, including spelling, can be found in great abundance. Even music can profitably be brought in on these days.

Should there be a desire to have a program for one of these special days, one can be easily made, beforehand, from reference and material found in this book.

Have some of the scholars, the day before, tastefully drape the room with bunting, flags, pictures, mottoes or flowers appropriate to the day you celebrate. Nothing is prettier or more pleasing to the eye and ambition, than to have on the blackboards appropriate drawings, drawn by the scholars of the room.

REMARKS.

The St. Paul Board of Education, two years ago, moved that the United States flag should float over each public school building during the entire school session, or school year, and taken down at the close of the school year; but was to be raised, during the vacation time, on a legal holiday. In the school report of the Board of Education of Minneapolis of 1897, it says, in Sec. 32, that, "On the days designated by the Superintendent for the raising of flags, the principal shall see that the duty be attended to by the janitor, unless, in his judgment, the severity of the weather should make such raising undesirable."

All the public schools of Minneapolis and St. Paul are named after some of our most prominent presidents, poets, generals and benevolent men.

Election Day is not a flag day, but is a legal holiday in most of the states. It generally occurs on the first Tuesday after the first Monday in November of every even year.

During the war with Spain, 1898, by vote of the Board of Education of Minneapolis, the flags on all the public schools were raised for an indefinite time.

Arbor Day, Labor Day, Good Friday and Thanksgiving Day are not flag days in Minneapolis, but are observed as holidays, and the flags are raised, except on Good Friday.

CONTENTS.

			Page.
Jan.	1.	Emancipation Proclamation,	11
Jan.	1.	New Year's Day,	15
Jan.	12.	Invention of Telegraph,	17
Feb.	12.	Lincoln's Birthday,	19
Feb.	22.	Washington's Birthday,	21
Feb.	22.	Lowell's Birthday,	23
Feb.	27.	Longfellow's Birthday,	25
Mar.	9.	Engagement Between Monitor and Merrimac,	27
April	9.	Surrender of Appomatax,	29
April	15.	Death of Lincoln, (Half-mast),	30
April	19.	Battle of Lexington,	34
April	—.	Arbor Day,	36
April	30.	Inauguration of First President of U. S.,	38
May	11.	Minnesota Admitted as a State, 1858,	40
May	30.	Memorial Day, (Half-mast),	42
June	17.	Battle of Bunker Hill,	44
July	3.	Battle of Gettysburg,	46
July	4.	Declaration of Independence,	49
July	23.	Establishment of First School in St. Paul,	51
Sept.	6.	Labor Day,	53
Sept.	9.	Discovery of St. Anthony Falls,	54
Sept.	19.	Death of Garfield, (Half-mast.)	56
Oct.	12.	Discovery of America,	60
Oct.	19.	Surrender of Cornwallis,	64
Nov.	19.	Establishment 1st Public School in Mpls.,	67
Nov.	—.	Thanksgiving Day,	70
Dec.	17.	Whittier's Birthday,	71
Dec.	22.	Landing of Pilgrims,	73
Dec.	25.	Christmas,	76
		References,	78
		Notes,	79

JANUARY FIRST.
Emancipation Proclamation.

During the summer of 1862, President Lincoln prepared the original draft which was to set free all slaves within the borders of the Confederate States. But, owing to the Union reverses, he laid it aside, stating, "That when a victory came he would issue it." Still things looked dark to the Unionists. Finally the Battle of Antietam was fought, and as the advantage was on our side, President Lincoln finished writing the second draft, September 22, 1862, while staying at the Soldiers' Home.

He then called the members of his cabinet together, presented it, and said, "I made a solemn vow before God, that if General Lee was driven back from Maryland, I would crown the result by the declaration of freedom to the slaves."

President Lincoln had prayed most earnestly to God about this matter, and after the most calm and careful deliberation, made up his mind that, in order to save the Union, he must free mankind; and now as he was placed in a position to do so, and as it only required a stroke of his pen, he would do it and thus free a whole race for all time to come.

So, January 1, 1863, New Year's Day, was signalized by the issue of the Emancipation Proclamation which declared "slavery at an end throughout all parts of the country that might be in rebellion against the United States." Thus 4,000,000 people were set free.

You will notice that President Lincoln's signature to the Proclamation appears somewhat tremulous and uneven. When asked the reason for this, the President replied: "Not because of any uncertainty or hesitation on my part, but it was just after the public reception, and three hours' handshaking is not calculated to improve a man's chirography."

The following is a copy of the complete Proclamation:

"Whereas, on the twenty-second day of September, in the

year of our Lord one thousand eight hundred and sixty-two, a proclamation was issued by the President of the United States, containing, among other things, the following, to-wit:

"'That on the first day of January, in the year of our Lord one thousand eight hundred and sixty-three, all persons held as slaves within any State, or designated part of a State, the people whereof shall then be in rebellion against the United States, shall be then, thenceforth and forever free, and the Executive Government of the United States, including the military and naval authorities thereof, will recognize and maintain the freedom of such persons, and will do no act or acts to repress such persons, or any of them, in any efforts they may make for their actual freedom.

"'That the Executive will, on the first day of January aforesaid, by proclamation, designate the States and parts of States, if any, in which the people therein respectively shall then be in rebellion against the United States, and the fact that any State, or the people thereof, shall on that day be in good faith represented in the Congress of the United States, by members chosen thereto at elections wherein a majority of the qualified voters of such States shall have participated, shall, in the absence of strong countervailing testimony, be deemed conclusive evidence that such State or the people thereof are not then in rebellion against the United States.'

"Now, therefore, I, Abraham Lincoln, President of the United States, by virtue or the power in me vested as Commander-in-chief of the Army and Navy of the United States in time of actual armed rebellion against the authority and Government of the United States, and as a fit and necessary war measure for suppressing said rebellion, do, on the first day of January, in the year of our Lord one thousand eight hundred and sixty-three, and in accordance with my purpose so to do, publicly proclaimed for the full period of one hundred days of the first above mentioned order, designate as the States and parts of States wherein the people thereof respectively are this day in rebellion against the United States the following, to-wit: Arkansas, Texas, Louisiana, except the parishes of St. Bernard,

Plaquemines, Jefferson, St. John, St. Charles, St. James, Ascension, Assumption, Terre Bonne, Lafourche, St. Mary, St. Martin, and Orleans, including the City of New Orleans; Mississippi, Alabama, Florida, Georgia, South Carolina, North Carolina and Virginia, except the forty-eight counties designated as West Virginia, and also the counties of Berkeley, Accomac, Northampton, Elizabeth City, York, Princess Ann and Norfolk, including the cities of Norfolk and Portsmouth, and which excepted parts are, for the present, left precisely as if this Proclamation were not issued.

"And by virtue of the power and for the purpose aforesaid, I do order and declare that all persons held as slaves within said designated States and parts of States are, and henceforward shall be, free; and that the Executive Government of the United States, including the military and naval authorities thereof, will recognize and maintain the freedom of such persons.

"And I hereby enjoin upon the people so declared to be free to abstain from all violence, unless in necessary self-defence, and I recommend to them that in all cases, when allowed, they labor faithfully for reasonable wages.

"And I further declare and make known that such persons of suitable condition will be received into the armed service of the United States to garrison forts, positions, stations and other places, and to man vessels of all sorts in said service.

"And upon this, sincerely believed to be an act of justice, warranted by the Constitution, upon military necessity, I invoke the considerate judgment of mankind and the gracious favor of Almighty God.

"In witness whereof I have hereunto set my hand and caused the seal of the United States to be affixed.

"Done at the City of Washington, this first day of January, in the year of our Lord one thousand eight hundred and (L. S.) sixty-three, and of the Independence of the United States of America the eighty-seventh."

"By the President:
                    "ABRAHAM LINCOLN."
"WILLIAM H. SEWARD, Secretary of State."

In January, 1865, Congress finally voted for an amendment to the Constitution which is consecrated by the 13th, abolishing slavery; and by the end of the year this had been approved by an overwhelming majority of the State Legislatures.

"Art. XII., Sec. I.: Neither slavery nor involuntary servitude, except as a punishment for crime whereof the party shall have been duly convicted, shall exist within the United States or any place subject to their jurisdiction."

Also the right to vote as citizens was given to the poor negroes by Congress.

"Art. XV., Sec. I.: The right of the citizens of the United States to vote shall not be denied or abridged by the United States, or by any State, on account of race, color, or previous condition of servitude."

JANUARY FIRST.
New Year's Day.

The celebration of the commencement of New Year's Day by some religious observance, accompanied by festive rejoicing, dates from high antiquity. The Jews, the Egyptians, the Chinese, the Romans and the Mohammedans all regarded it as a day of special interest, although differing as to the time of the celebration.

The Jews celebrated it as the anniversary of Adam's birthday, and still continue to do so at the present time, with splendid entertainments.

The Romans made this a holiday and dedicated it to Janus, with rich and numerous sacrifices. Janus was a Latin deity, having two faces, looking in opposite directions. In times ot war his temple doors were kept open; in times of peace, closed. It is recorded that the gates were kept open eight times. Romulus is said to have founded the temple.

All newly elected magistrates entered upon their offices on this day, and the people made presents of gilt figs, dates and plums to their friends, the Emperor also receiving presents from his subjects, which became later compulsory to give.

On the establishing of Christianity, the usage of a solemn inauguration of the New Year was retained; but, as to the manner of observing it, and to the time of observation, it differed greatly. Sometimes the celebration of Christmas Day, or the 25th of March, Annunciation Day, Easter Day, or the 1st of March, would share with the 1st of January.

It was not till late in the 16th century that the 1st of January was universally accepted as the first day of the new year.

The early fathers, Chrysostom, Ambrose, Augustine and others, prohibited the Christians the use of all festive celebrations, stating that they were paganish; but, on the contrary, substituted prayer, fasting and humiliation for the opening of the

Christian year. This was partially observed, and is to the present day. But the festival and social character predominated then and now.

In many countries the night of New Year's Eve, "St. Sylvester's Eve," was celebrated with great festivity till twelve o'clock, when, with congratulations, complimentary visits and mutual wishes for a "Happy New Year," the new year was ushered in. This is an ancient Scottish custom, prevailing in Germany also.

The practice of tolling the bells at midnight and ringing the new year in is still observed in many places. The custom of celebrating the New Year's Day by calling on friends, making New Year's calls, we owe to the Dutch; but this custom is rapidly falling into desuetude.

New Year's Day is a legal holiday in all states except Kentucky, Massachusetts, Mississippi, New Hampshire and Rhode Island.

JANUARY TWELFTH.
Invention of Telegraph.

Samuel F. B. Morse, LL. D., an artist, inventor and eldest son of Rev. J. Morse, D. D., was born at Charleston, Mass., April 27, 1791. He graduated from Yale College and in 1810 studied portrait painting in Europe with Washington Allston and Benjamin West. Received, in 1813, a gold medal for his artistic work. Among his paintings is a full length portrait of Gen. Lafayette.

On returning to New York he founded the National Academy of Design, in 1825, and became its first president, and professor of arts and designs. After his second visit to Europe, he became discouraged in regard to his paintings and, during twelve years of poverty, he pursued his studies on the properties of the "electro magnet," and chemistry, and more than once had great hopes of his invention.

He went to France to witness the electrical experiments in Paris; and on his return home in company with his friend, Prof. Jackson, a word dropped during their conversation that took deep hold of Morse, and he proposed, to himself, to develop the idea, and, before the end of the voyage, he had drawn out the general plan of the system that now bears his name. He could hardly wait till he reached home, so anxious was he to give it a trial.

January 12, upon a wire half a mile in length, he tried his experiment and found it worked nicely.

In 1837 he applied for a patent for his magnetic telegraph, but did not receive it until 1840. He petitioned Congress for money to experiment, at a distance, with his telegraph, but was refused. He then applied to England, but was also refused.

In 1843, as he had almost given up in despair of ever receiving anything in the way of help. Congress, at midnight, and in the last moments of the session, appropriated $30,000 for an experimental line between Washington, D. C., and Baltimore. The telegraph was tested on this line May 24, 1844, and revealed what has been called "the greatest triumph of human genius over space and time."

The first message sent over the wire, at a distance of forty miles, and at a cost of $30,000, was the proceedings of the convention that nominated Mr. Polk for the presidency of the United States.

For this telegraphic invention Morse was rewarded by testimonials, honors, orders of nobility, wealth, and was banqueted by Europe and America. Even the sovereigns of Europe presented him with $80,000.

Telegraphic wires soon threaded the country in all directions, from the Atlantic to the Pacific, and were soon introduced in all parts of the civilized world.

There are at present over a hundred thousand miles of telegraphic wire in operation, and the recording electric telegraph and Morse's alphabet are used on 95 per cent. of all the wires in the world.

Mr. Morse's alphabet is very simple, consisting of "dots and dashes marked by a steel pricker upon a sheet of paper, uncoiled beneath it by clock-work mechanism."

Mr. Morse's invention is the simplest of all electric telegraphs, as it only requires a single wire and is self-recording and printing.

In the United States there are over 125,564 miles of wire and the number of messages sent since its invention is over 12,000,000, at a cost of millions of dollars. The number of poles used for these wires per mile varies from twenty to twenty-two on minor lines, and from twenty-six to thirty on main lines.

The origination of the submarine telegraphy is also claimed by Mr. Morse. He took part in laying the first Atlantic cable in 1857.

Mr. Morse died in New York, April 2, 1872.

FEBRUARY TWELFTH.
Lincoln's Birthday.*

Called "Honest Abe," "The Railsplitter" and "The Martyr President." Motto: "With malice towards none and charity for all."

Abraham Lincoln, a tall, ungainly man, little versed in the refinements of society, but gifted by nature with great common sense, kind, earnest, sympathetic, faithful, democratic and only anxious to serve his country and mankind, was born of English ancestry in a little log-house in Hardin county, Ky., February 12, 1809. His father was very poor and was unable to read or write his own name, and his dear mother, and companion, died when Abe was quite young. So, all through his boyhood life Abe had nothing but hardships and toil, receiving only a very meager education, attending school less than a year during his whole life, although he had learned to read almost as soon as he had learned to walk.

After the death of his mother, 1818, his father married again, 1819, and Sally Bush was a good, faithful stepmother to little Abe and his sister, Sarah.

At eight years of age Abe's father moved to Indiana, the family floating down the Ohio river on a raft. Here Abe helped his father build a log-house and worked as a hired boy on a neighbor's farm. In 1830 the family moved again, going to Illinois, this time moving by means of a wagon driven by oxen. Here we find Abe splitting rails for a living, or working on a flatboat, or as a clerk in a country store; later a postmaster, surveyor, and finally captain of a company of volunteers in the Black Hawk War.

Abe was very fond of reading and studying and, although he had no time to do so in the day, he would do so in the quiet

*See Death of Lincoln and Emancipation Proclamation in this book.

hours of the night. In this way he studied law, borrowing books in the evening and returning them again in the morning. The very first book he read, when a boy, was the "Life of Washington."

He was finally admitted to the bar and began the practice of law in 1836. When twenty-five years old, he was elected a member of the Illinois Legislature, where he remained for a number of years, having been elected three times as a member. After this he was sent to Congress, where, on January 12, he made his first speech. From now on he rapidly rose to distinction, and finally, when they were looking around for a wise man for the President of the United States, as the country was in such a state of excitement about slavery, the people began to say: "Why not choose Abraham Lincoln of Illinois?" So, on May 16, 1860, Lincoln was nominated President of the United States, and was inaugurated March 4, 1861. The tone of his inaugural address was taken by the Secessionists as a challenge of war. War seemed inevitable and, in order to save the Union, Lincoln issued his Emancipation Proclamation, January 1, 1863, which set free all the slaves in the Union, and for this Lincoln lost his life, being shot by J. Wilkes Booth, April 14, 1865, while attending a play, on Friday evening, at Ford's Theater.

He died, in Washington, D. C., April 15, 1865, greatly beloved and mourned by all who knew him. It is said of him that "his wan, fatigued face and his bent form told of the cares he bore and the grief he felt." He was never known to smile, but was full of jokes which made others smile.

He married, November 4, 1842, Mary Todd, and had three children, all boys, only one of whom, Robt. T. Lincoln, of Chicago, Ill., is still living.

During the Civil War Lincoln called twelve times for volunteers, some to serve for three to six months, others for one, two and three years. In all he called for 2,942,748 and received 2,690,401.

Lincoln's Birthday is a legal holiday in the states of Illinois, Minnesota, New York, New Jersey, Washington, Connecticut, Pennsylvania and North Dakota.

FEBRUARY TWENTY-SECOND.

Washington's Birthday.*

Called "The Father of His Country."
Last Words: "I die hard; but I am not afraid to go."

George Washington, the commander-in-chief of the American forces in the Revolutionary War, the president of the convention that framed the Constitution of the United States, the hero of Valley Forge and Yorktown, and the first President of the United States, was born of wealthy English parentage, in Westmoreland county, Va., February 12, 1732.

In early life, George was well trained in truthfulness, outdoor exercises and education. At the age of twelve, George's dear father died, leaving George, his mother and four brothers well provided for. At the age of thirteen, George wrote, for his own use, one hundred and ten maxims of civility and good behavior; and, at fourteen years old, he wanted to go to sea and take part in the war between France and Spain. His mother had his trunk packed and the British vessel was ready to carry him away, when, on seeking his mother to bid her good-bye, he found her weeping for him. He being a brave, good boy, said, "O mother, mother, I will not go; I will stay with you until I am a grown up man," and he did.

In 1748 he showed great care and accuracy in surveying the grounds of Lord Fairfax. He was scarcely twenty-two years old when his country needed him, and his military genius was

---

*See Inauguration of first President of the United States, Surrender of Cornwallis and the Declaration of Independence in this book.

greatly shown in the French and Indian War of America.

In 1759 he married Mrs. Martha Curtiss, a rich widow lady. He now resigned his military appointments to become a country gentleman, owning a large plantation and one hundred and twenty-five slaves. In his will it is stated that his slaves should have their freedom after his and his wife's death. His wife died three years after her husband.

George Washington was a man a little over six feet in height, had brown hair, blue eyes, large head and strong arms; was an athlete, a bold, graceful rider and hunter; was gracious, gentle, cool, reserved and truthful. He was very dignified and paid great attention to his personal appearance; was childless, but had very happy domestic relations.

He was elected to the House of Burgesses and later to the General Congress at Philadelphia, and until the crisis at Lexington had opposed most strongly the separation from England, but when war was inevitable, in June, 1775, he gladly acquiesced to become the commander-in-chief of the newly-formed army, and although discouraged and defeated many times, he proved himself "first in war."

Through the help of the French troops, in 1781, Washington compelled the surrender of Cornwallis at Yorktown, practically putting an end to the Revolutionary War.

After the adoption of the Federal Constitution he was elected the first President of the United States, and after a prosperous administration of eight years he retired to his home at Mt. Vernon, where he died December 14, 1799.

He was greatly mourned by all, even his enemies, and he well deserves the record of being "first in peace, first in war and first in the hearts of his countrymen."

Washington's Birthday is a legal holiday in all states except Arkansas, Iowa and Mississippi.

FEBRUARY TWENTY-SECOND.

Lowell's Birthday.

James R. Lowell, an American poet, who was most admired by the English people, was born in the delightful old Revolutionary parsonage of Elmwood, Cambridge, Mass., February 22, 1819.

His family consisted of great and good men. His mother, a good woman, later became insane. Lowell wrote a poem on "The Darkened Mind," which refers to his dearly beloved mother.

Lowell was the youngest of five children, had a happy childhood, and after a brief experience in a district school, was sent to a boys' academy in Cambridge. Here he received the greater part of his education; until, at the age of sixteen, he entered Harvard College.

Lowell spent most of his time in the family library reading, as he did not care for his studies. At an early age he began to write poetry and was appointed class poet while in college. He liked to write rhymes better than he liked to study, and his father, fearing he would neglect his studies for his poetry, begged James not to write any more; so, to please his father, he gave up writing, studied harder and graduated from Harvard, then began the study of law. He was admitted to the bar in 1840, practiced a short time and then gave it up for his literary calling.

In 1844 he married Maria White, a beautiful, cultured and poetical woman. "The Alpine Sheep" and "The Morning Glory" are poems written by her. They had several children; all died except a little girl, who lived to grow up to womanhood. His poems, "The Changeling" and "The First Snow Fall," are about his little children.

In 1851 he and his wife went to Europe to study. On returning home he devoted himself to his literary work, writing many funny stories about slavery, which attracted much attention. These are called the "Bigelow Papers."

One of his best poems is "The Vision of Sir Launfal," written in less than two days, and during which time he neither ate nor slept. It teaches us noble lessons of true charity.

In his poem, "The Fable for Critics," he describes, very kindly, Longfellow's, Whittier's, Bryant's and many other poets' (including himself) manner of writing. "After the Burial" is a poem written by Lowell, showing his great sorrow for his dearly beloved wife, who had recently died.

As Lowell was appointed to succeed Longfellow as professor in Harvard College, he went to Europe to prepare himself for his work. On returning home he married another charming woman, Francis Dunlap, who was very fond of his little daughter.

In 1857 he became the editor of the Atlantic Monthly and had great influence in public affairs during the Civil War. He wrote "The Commemoration Ode" during the war, and afterwards read it at the opening of the new hall which was built in memory of the many soldiers who died during the war.

After the war he led a quiet life at Elmwood, reading, writing, walking and taking care of his garden, until he was called into public life by being appointed Minister to Spain in 1877 and later to England in 1880. While in England, he was welcomed and honored by all who knew him.

On the death of his wife, he returned to America and lived with his daughter and her children at Elmwood, lecturing now and then at Cambridge. He died at Cambridge in 1891.

Lowell was not obliged to write for a living, as he had plenty of money, but did so because he loved to write, had the talents, and thought it his duty and aim to make men better. It is said of him that "he knew the songs of every bird, so familiar was he with them, also the names of the flowers and where each grew."

FEBRUARY TWENTY-SEVENTH.

Longfellow's Birthday.

Called "The Children's Poet."

Henry W. Longfellow, the most popular of American poets, and considered the most famous American translator of Dante, was born in Portland, Me., February 27, 1807. He is a descendant of the famous Puritan, Priscilla.

At the age of fourteen, he entered Bowdoin College and graduated four years after. He then entered his father's law office and began the study of law, but as he had been offered the professorship of foreign language and literature at Bowdoin College, he went to Europe to prepare himself better for his duties.

He was married twice; first, in 1831, to Miss Potter, who was burned to death while in Europe in 1835, and second, in 1843, to Francis Appleton, who was the mother of his five children.

His literary work began when he was quite young, and increased in value and thought as he grew older. Many of his poems are from a personal standpoint, and are valuable as such, although the imaginative poems are very attractive. It is said or him that "he was free from the faults of many literary men; his serene and amiable disposition never subjected him to envy or jealousy."

Washington's old headquarters at Cambridge was where Longfellow spent most of his time, while in America, and did most of his writing, even up to the time of his death. He died here March 24, 1882.

Among his many friends are found such men as Emerson,

Hawthorne, Holmes, Lowell and Agassiz, of whom he has written much. Among his writings are: "Evangeline," "Hiawatha," "Courtship of Miles Standish," "Voices of the Night," "Tales of a Wayside Inn," "Excelsior," "Building of the Ship," "Poems on Slavery," "The Psalm of Life," "Outre Mer," "Hyperion," "The Spanish Student" and "Paul Revere's Ride."

In 1882 the school children of the city of Albany, N. Y., each contributed ten cents towards a beautiful monument to their dear poet's memory. Each child received a beautiful steel-engraved card with a verse and the poet's picture on, and were to have their names inscribed on the poet's monument.

MARCH NINTH.

Engagement Between Monitor and Merrimac.

Thirty-five years ago, in Hampton Roads, the most remarkable naval battle was fought between the Monitor and the Merrimac, March 9, 1863.

The Merrimac, the Confederate vessel, was made of heavy oak timber, covered with old railroad iron, and formed a roof-like house; a ram of oak and iron, thirty-three feet long, projected from a heavy false bow. She carried four eighty-pound rifle cannon, and was commanded by Capt. Buchanan. The Monitor, or "Yankee Cheese Box," as it was called, was commanded by Lieut. John L. Worden, and had just been built by Captain Ericsson. It was the first one of its kind, and was a flat-bottomed float, one hundred and twenty-four feet long, with a deck a few inches above the water, and carried a curious revolving tower in the center. It was made of wood, covered with iron, the deck and turret-roof being bomb-proof. It carried two 168-pound guns, which it could turn in any direction it wished, and the smokestack could be lowered out of harm's way when necessary. It had an artificial means of ventilation, which admitted the air, but prevented the water from coming in. It was only one-fifth the size of the Merrimac, and its burden was 900 tons.

During the beginning of March, the Confederate iron-clad, Merrimac, had been playing havoc with the Union fleet, destroying everything that came in its way. But on the morning of the 9th of March, 1863, as the Merrimac steamed out of its harbor at Norfolk into Hampton Roads to destroy the Union fleet which was there, it encountered an unexpected, queer looking antagonist, which hurled its monster two 168-pound balls into the Merrimac. This was the "Cheese Box" Monitor.

The Merrimac returned the salute with force, that, had it been another vessel, would have doomed it, but as it was, the Confederate balls only rattled harmlessly on the deck of the little Monitor, doing no harm.

The Merrimac finding this of no avail, ran close against the Monitor, and for five hours they exchanged heavy volleys of shot and shell. Five times did the Merrimac try to run down the Monitor with her huge iron beak, but it only grated over the deck of the Monitor. Every time the Monitor would glide gracefully out unharmed.

The Merrimac, now finding that she could do nothing with her doughty little antagonist, and as she was getting the worst of it, gave up the fight and steamed back to Norfolk so disabled that she was never used again.

While steaming away, she let fly a shot which struck the Monitor's pilot house, breaking an iron bar nine by twelve inches and seriously injuring the eyes of Lieut. Worden, the gallant commander, who was at that moment peering out through a narrow slit directing the firing of his guns.

The battle was a great victory for the Unionist, and on it hinged the war.

APRIL NINTH.

Surrender of Appomatox.

After a long and gallant contest, with his resolute and able adversary, General Robt. E. Lee, with only the wreck of his proud array of soldiers who had dealt the Union army so many crushing blows during the Civil War, surrendered the Confederate army to General Grant at Appomattox Court House April 9, 1865, an event which caused the greatest joy throughout the North and eventually put a stop to the Civil War.

General Lee, after abandoning Petersburg and Richmond, which the Union army took possession of, retreated westward, hoping to join Johnston in North Carolina, but was hotly pursued by the combined forces of Grant and Sheridan. Several partial engagements were fought during their long race, and at one time it seemed as if it would end in one of the bloodiest tragedies of the Civil War. Lee, on finding that his army was completely surrounded by the Union forces and that further advances were out of the question, accepted the terms which General Grant had already sent, demanding the surrender of Appomattox. The terms were: "That the officers and men were allowed to go home on their paroles not to take up arms against the United States, and the officers were to retain their private baggage and horses." Many of the soldiers rode their own horses, so were allowed to keep them to help them in their future work at home.

So the remains of the grand army of Virginia, consisting of about 8,000 men, laid down their arms near Appomattox Court House and then homeward turned, "no longer Confederate soldiers, but American citizens."

By the end of May of the same year all the Confederate forces had surrendered and the War of 1861 was a thing of the past.

APRIL FIFTEENTH.

Death of Lincoln.*

Called "The Saviour" and "The Liberator of a Race."
President Lincoln appointed the 14th of April, 1865, as a day of thanksgiving, it being the anniversary of the surrender of Fort Sumpter.

Every arrangement was being made to make it a glorious event, and Major Anderson, who so nobly defended the United States flag, was to raise again the old tattered emblem that the rebels had compelled him to haul down just four years ago.

The nation was filled with joy at the prospect, and distinguished men, as Grant and Colfax, were to be present. No one felt more devoutly thankful than did President Lincoln. The terrible war was over and peace and harmony were now going to prevail.

President Lincoln took breakfast with his son, Robert T., who had witnessed the surrender of General Lee to General Grant, and was relating all the particulars, which were very interesting to his father. Later on, President Lincoln met General Grant and they talked matters over. After this meeting the President made arrangements to attend the theater in the evening, this being a favorite pastime of the President's when very tired.

He talked pleasantly with his wife during the day about the terrible storm of war he had passed through, and of the bright and peaceful future dawning upon him. When evening

*See his Life and Proclamation in this book.

came, President Lincoln found that General Grant had to leave town, so he invited Major Rathbone, Senator Harris and daughter to accompany him to the theater. Lincoln said "he would be glad to stay at home, but as the audience were expecting both General Grant and himself, he did not like to disappoint them altogether." So he went, sacrificing himself to please others. About eight o'clock his carriage came and he and his wife drove off for their guests, and then proceeded to Ford's Theater. The play was, "The American Cousin."

The President sat in a high rocking chair with his back to the door, in the corner of the box nearest to the audience. The door of the box was guarded by a messenger outside and was situated on the second floor. It, as well as the whole building, was prettily draped with American flags. About half past ten, J. Wilkes Booth, an actor and fanatical secessionist, came along the passageway, showed his card to the messenger, who allowed him to pass by. Booth stepped in the vestibule of the President's box, shut and barred the door quietly, then stealing stealthily up behind the President's chair, drew a small silver-mounted pistol and shot the President through the back of the head. The President never uttered a sound. Everybody that heard the report thought it was some part of the play, except Major Rathbone, who saw through the smoke a man, and attempted to seize him, but Booth stabbed him in the shoulder with a long, double-edged dagger. As soon as he had done this, Booth rushed to the front of the box, brandished his dagger and shouting, "Sic semper tyrannis," which meant, "Thus ever to tyrants." He then leaped, shouting, "The South is avenged," from the box to the stage, and in so doing, his spur caught in the American flag, "a mute avenger of the nation's chief," and he fell, breaking his leg. Darting as quickly as he could behind the scenes, he escaped through a back door and out into the street; jumping on a horse that was waiting for him, he rode rapidly into Maryland. He was at length overtaken in a barn, and as he would not surrender himself, the building was fired to drive him out, but he remained inside and was shot from without by the soldiers.

The accomplices of Booth were arrested, tried and convicted. Harrold, Payne, Atzerott and Mrs. Surratt were hanged July 7, 1865; Arnold, Mudd and McLaughlin imprisoned for life, while Spangler was sentenced for six years. The ropes which these prisoners were hanged with are to be seen at Libby Prison, Chicago; also the blood-stained sheets and bed on which Lincoln had lain.

The President was removed to a house on the opposite side of the street and physicians and surgeons were summoned, but the wound was mortal. Twenty-two minutes past seven Saturday morning, April 15, 1865, Abraham Lincoln passed from this world into the next, where his reward awaited him.

At the same time as the assassination of President Lincoln, Secretary Seward and the other cabinet officers were in danger of their lives, as the villain had planned to rid the country of all the high officials.

The death of Lincoln was a national one. It seemed as if a dear friend lay dead in every house. Everything seemed to stand still and black bunting and flags were seen flying everywhere.

Directly after his death, his body was embalmed and carried to the White House and placed in the green room. It remained there till Wednesday, when it was placed in the east room, where the Episcopal services were read. After these simple services, his body was escorted by a stately train to the capitol, where thousands of people came to take the last fond look at their beloved "Martyred Chief." The whole immense building, from the ground to the dome of the capitol, inside and out, was heavily draped in mourning.

His remains, together with those of his beloved son, Willie, were then removed to Springfield, Ill., their former home.

A magnificent funeral car was prepared, and a guard was selected from the Veterans' Reserve Corps, which, with a large company of invited gentlemen, formed the escort. The engine and train were draped in black, and the rate of speed was restricted. A pilot engine steamed ahead to prevent accident. This great funeral procession passed over a distance of more than a thousand miles, passing through large cities, thus allowing the people to gaze upon the martyred dead.

Thus, he who a little more than four years ago was comparatively an unknown man, and who was obliged to enter Washington in disguise, under the cover of night, for fear of assassination, now went forth, a mighty conqueror, his pathway of a thousand miles strewn with the rarest flowers and bedewed with a nation's tears.

He was laid to rest in Oak Ridge cemetery, May 4, 1865, mourned not only by his own country, but by England, France, Russia, Italy, Prussia, Belgium, Turkey, Austria, Switzerland and many other civilized countries.

APRIL NINETEENTH.

Battle of Lexington.

The first blood shed in the Revolutionary War was on April 19, 1775, at Lexington, a little town about ten miles northwest of Boston, on the road to Concord.

The patriots had collected stores of ammunition at Concord, and it was the object of the British to destroy these, and to capture Samuel Adams and John Hancock, both of whom were regarded as "Arch Rebels."

So in the still of the night, April 18th, the British, commanded by Lieut.-Col. Smith, marched out of Boston, on their way to Concord, making no noise. They did not intend that the Americans should know that they were coming. Nevertheless the Americans discovered it and Dr. Warren sent Paul Revere across the Charles River at midnight, to tell the country people the British were coming.

The news sped like the wind. Guns were fired, bells rang and drums beat; and every man and boy, old or young, filled their pockets with bullets, and were ready to fight.

Capt. Parker had told his men, these farmer boys, not to fire first, but wait and see what the regulars would do; besides, the poor Americans didn't have ammunition enough.

About four o'clock in the morning, April 19, 1775, Thad Bowman, an American patriot, rode furiously up to the Commons, and cried out: "Here they come. The British are coming!"

The order was given by Capt. Parker to beat the drums, and the British took this as a challenge. In a moment 800 British soldiers marched in sight of the Americans' little band of less than 100, and at double quick time advanced, shouting and firing.

The Americans were ordered to lay down their arms, and on their disregarding this order, were fired upon by the British. The Americans returned the fire. Several men were killed and wounded. One of our brave men, named Jonas Parker, said he would never run from the regulars, and he never did; even after he was wounded he fought like a tiger, until a cowardly red-coat ran him through with a bayonet.

The British again took up their march towards Concord, where they took possession of the village and destroyed the stores; such stores of ammunition as they could find, as the greater part of them had already been removed by the American patriots. At night it was found that the British had lost 73 killed, 174 wounded and 26 missing; while the Americans lost 49 killed, 39 wounded and five missing. Two hundred and seventy-three to ninety-three. It was not a bad beginning for the American farmer boys, who had never been trained in military tactics.

On a monument which stands near this battle scene of 1775, are these words written by Emerson:

"By the rude bridge that arched the flood,
Their flag to April's breeze unfurled,
Here once the embattled farmer stood,
And fired the shot heard round the world."

The anniversary of the battle of Lexington, April 19, is observed as a legal holiday in Massachusetts each year.

APRIL.

Arbor Day.

To ex-Gov. J. Sterling Morton, of Nebraska, the honor of originating Arbor Day belongs. For what with the endless prairies and the woodman's ax, man and animal life would have been unbearable had it not been for Mr. Morton's happy thought of remedying these conditions. So, at his suggestion "that the school children be allowed to plant trees and flowers once a year," a proclamation, the first of its kind, was issued in Nebraska in the year 1872 for the observance of such a day.

Over 12,000,000 trees were planted on the plains of Nebraska that year, and the next year it was enacted in the laws as a legal holiday for the purpose of setting out orchards, forests, ornamental trees and flowers.

Premiums and medals were also awarded to those who set out the greatest number of trees that day. So the prairies of Nebraska, extending for over three hundred miles west of the Missouri River, are provided to-day with over 600,000,000 trees, where only a few years ago nothing in the way of a tree could be seen in these parts, except along the streams.

The grand example which Nebraska set has been followed by her sister states, Kansas being the first to observe it, others soon following.

In 1876 Arbor Day was first observed in Minnesota, and over a million and a half of trees were set out on that day.

At the National Educational Convention of 1886 it was unanimously adopted. "That all states should have an Arbor Day."

This day is set apart for the purpose of planting trees and flowers, and is generally appointed by the governor of that state, the time differing in each state.

Beginning with the second week in February, Arbor Day is observed in the Southern States, and in March, April and May in the Middle, Western and Northern. In Minnesota it is usually observed the latter part of April of each year.

It is the custom of the school children to plant trees or flowers on the school grounds, and then name them after some poet, especially those whose works have the love of nature in them. Such poets are Lucy Larcom, Celia Thaxter, Alice Cary, Lowell, Longfellow, Holmes, Bryant and Whittier.

Whittier speaks of the white ash, arbutus and palm; Holmes of the maple and elm; Lowell of the birch, willow, elm, oak, pine and violets; the Cary sisters of the basswood; Bryant of the oak, apple and yew; Longfellow of the maple; Emerson of the ironwood, while Dickens speaks of the ivy and Burns of the daisy.

The ages of trees vary, yet all seem to live a long time. The elm lives over 300 years, the maple 355 years, while the spruce, oak and yew live thousands of years.

The state flower of Minnesota is the "Bitter-root."

APRIL THIRTIETH.

Inauguration of First President of the United States.

The next step after the Constitution had been approved by the requisite number of states, was to choose a president and a vice-president.

From one end of the country to the other came the voice, "Washington is the father of his country. He defended us in times of danger; he will preserve us in times of peace."

A messenger came and told him, soon after, "That all hearts turned instinctively to him and that he was the unanimous choice of the people for President of the United States."

Washington regretted deeply having to leave his quiet home at Mt. Vernon for the tumult of political life, but he felt it his duty to do so again.

In those days there were no railroads, so Washington had to be driven to the seat of government, which was then in the City of New York. So he got in his beautiful coach, which was driven by several splendid horses, and drove to the capitol, where he was to take the oath of office.

On his way to New York, every city and village through which he had to pass was decorated with flags, flowers, and even arches. Cannon were fired, bells rang, and crowds greeted him everywhere. Fathers shouted, mothers wept, young maidens sang songs of rejoicing and children strewed flowers in his pathway.

All these demonstrations filled the heart of Washington with gratitude and thankfulness for the past and hope for the future of his country.

On the balcony of the old Federal Hall building, in the City of New York, Washington took the oath of office to support the Constitution of the United States.

This old site is the present site of the Subtreasury building of the United States. Here, also, was organized the Federal Congress, which was to take the place of the old Continental Congress that had carried the nation successfully through its eight years of war.

So on the 30th of April, 1789, Washington was inaugurated the first President of the United States. He was elected for four years, and when his term expired the people elected him again, and would gladly have elected him a third time, but he refused to serve any longer.

John Adams was chosen Vice-President, and the members of Washington's cabinet were Thomas Jefferson, Alexander Hamilton, Major-General Henry Knox and Edmund Randolph, all able and learned men.

MAY ELEVENTH.

Minnesota Admitted as a State.

Minnesota was the nineteenth territory that applied for admission to the Union. She was admitted May 11, 1858, being the seventh of the Northwestern States to ask for admission.

The State of Minnesota was a part of the vast region of Louisiana, which the United States purchased from France in 1813, having been first explored by Father Hennepin over two centuries ago.

The first settlement made in this French territory was at the mouth of the Pigeon River, in 1678, by Daniel Greysolon du Luth.

After the acquisition of this vast territory by the United States, Lieut. Pike was sent by the Governor, in 1805, to explore this region. He succeeded in getting as far as Sandy and Leech Lakes.

In 1812 another settlement was made by a party from Red River County, British possessions, and in 1819 Fort Snelling was established by the Government. Where the flourishing City of St. Paul now stands there were only two or three little log cabins, built by a small colony of Swiss people from Winnipeg, in 1838.

After eleven years, or in 1849, while this region was a vast wilderness, over which the Sioux and other Indians roamed, it was organized into a territory by the Government. It had a population of less than five thousand people, made up of whites and half-breeds, who were found around the various trading posts and missions.

Alexander Ramsey was appointed their Territorial Governor in 1849, and Henry H. Sibley the first State Governor.

The Indians, in 1851, ceded all their land west of the Mississippi, as far as the Sioux River, to the United States, and from that time on the population increased so rapidly that in six years the territory applied to the Union for admission as a State.

Minnesota is so called from the river that bears its name, and signifies "cloudy or sky-tinted waters." It has an area of 83,365 square miles, with 81 counties, 133 or more rivers, 217 lakes, and over 1,301,826 inhabitants—there being about 900 Chippewa Indians, 400 Finns, besides many Laplanders, Russians, Danes, Scandinavians and Icelanders.

In 1849 the Arms of the State was devised. It shows the St. Anthony Falls in the distance, a plowman on the prairie plowing, while fleeing toward the setting sun is a mounted Indian.

The motto of the State is, "L'Etoile Du Nord," which means, "Star of the North."

St. Paul, settled in 1846 by emigrants from the East, is the capital, and is situated on terraces on the banks of the Mississippi River. It has immense manufacturing and railway interests.

Minneapolis, whose history begins with the building of the first house, by Col. John H. Stevens, on the west side of the Mississippi River near the Falls of St. Anthony in 1850, is the metropolis, and is situated on both sides of the Mississippi River. It has great railway shops, iron works, lumber and flour mills. Colonel Stevens' house was located about where the Union Depot now stands; but in the spring of 1896 the children of the public schools of Minneapolis moved this house to a permanent site in Minnehaha Park.

Duluth, the "Zenith City," ships immense quantities of flour and wheat over the great lakes to the East. Winona gathers the wheat from the southern part of Minnesota and ships it away.

Minnesota sent over 25,000 soldiers to the Civil War, and while her brave men were fighting at the front an Indian massacre occurred in the summer of 1862 at Fort Ripley and New Ulm. The Sioux Indians rose and cruelly killed over 800 helpless women and children. General Sibley was sent to drive the savages into Dakota, which he did, capturing 400 Indian warriors and 150 white people whom the Indians had captured. Of the 400 Indians, thirty-eight were hanged at Mankato as murderers. Their chief, "Little Crow," was killed.

MAY THIRTIETH.

Memorial Day.

The idea of decorating the soldiers' graves was first thought of in the Old World, and in the New World it was first observed in the South, where the Southern ladies decorated the graves of their fallen brave before the close of the hostilities of 1865.

Mrs. Henry S. Kimball, of West Philadelphia, Pa., while visiting in the South, in 1868, observed the pretty and appropriate custom among her Southern friends, and on returning to the North, wrote a letter to General John A. Logan, who was Commander-in-chief of the G. A. R., suggesting that we follow the same grand example set by our Southern sisters.

So impressed was General Logan with the noble idea, that he immediately sent an order out stating the idea suggested by Mrs. Kimball, and was greatly gratified when he saw how well it was received and practically adopted by the Grand Army of the Republic. He immediately wrote the following letter to Mrs. Kimball:

Washington, D. C., July 9, 1868.

"My Dear Friend—It is very gratifying to me to hear, as I do day after day from my friends, of the reception of my Order No. 11. As you observe, the custom is a beautiful one, and I am confident that it will not only never pass away from the recollection of the American people, but will more deeply ingraft itself in their hearts, and each returning anniversary of sacred decorations will increase in impressive devotion to our patriotic dead, and the crowns we weave for them of never fading laurels, and the beautiful flowers strewn over their graves, give birth to sentiments of love and of honor, which bind the past, the present and the future in one continuous chain of admiration, that the life and service of even the humblest private shall never be forgotten.

"Yours truly,
"JOHN A. LOGAN."

This holiday, though celebrated in a more quiet way than the Fourth of July, was first known as "Decoration Day" in the Northern States, but later as "Memorial Day."

It is not a national holiday, but forty-two states, including territories, have set apart a special day for decorating the soldiers' graves and holding appropriate services at their graves.

In thirty-five states this is observed on the 30th of May of each year, and if this day falls on a Sunday, the day before is observed, unless the day be another legal holiday.

In the year 1878, on June 1, at Springfield, Mass., the following resolution was adopted by the National Encampment: "Resolved, That all flags hoisted on 'Memorial Day' be at half mast." This signifies mourning; and when the flag is carried in the procession on Memorial Day it is draped in honor of the soldiers who fell defending the flag.

JUNE SEVENTEENTH.

Battle of Bunker Hill.

Bunker Hill is situated in the eastern part of Charlestown, Mass. It is about 110 feet high and is connected by a ridge to Breed's Hill, an elevation about seventy-five feet high.

These heights are memorable as being the seat of the first real battle fought for American Independence, June 17, 1775. Colonel Prescott, the American patriot, was sent, on the evening of June 16, with a troop of 1,500 men, to fortify Bunker Hill, but, on finding its height, he concluded to fortify Breed's Hill instead.

When dawn came the 3,000 British were amazed to see the intrenchments the Americans had thrown up during the night, and began cannonading the Americans immediately.

This failing to do what it was intended it should, 3,000 men, under General Howe, were sent to dislodge the patriots. Twice did the British approach within a few rods, but each time they were repulsed with heavy loss. At last, General Clinton arriving with reinforcements, the third charge was more successful.

The Americans had but a scanty supply of powder; it being said that there was less than fourteen barrels of powder in the whole American army on the day of the battle; so, Colonel Prescott told his men not to fire until they saw the whites of their enemies' eyes. When the powder did give out the Americans fought bravely with their muskets in a hand-to-hand battle.

Finally the Americans were forced to retreat, and, although the British gained the hill, the victory to them was more disastrous and humiliating than an ordinary defeat; while it was a glorious day for the Americans, and the defeat had the effect of a triumph to them.

The British lost, in killed and wounded, 1,054 men, while the Americans lost only 452 men. Among the Americans who were slain was the distinguished patriot, General Joseph Warren, who was President of the Provincial Congress of Massachusetts. General Howe valued this general at the worth of 500 common rebels. Major Pitcairn, a noted British officer, was also killed.

Before the Battle of Bunker Hill, General Gage sent an officer to the American camp, stating that he would pardon all American rebels who would lay down their arms; but our revolutionary fathers were not made of the back-down material, but were noted for their bravery and loyalty to the cause they espoused, and refused the British offer.

Near the spot, on Breed's Hill, where General Warren fell, stands the magnificent Bunker Hill Monument, the corner stone of which was laid June 17, 1825, by the noble and brave Marquis de Lafayette, who did so much for the independence of America.

JULY THIRD.

Battle of Gettysburg.

As the North was being threatened by an invasion from the Confederate troops under General Lee, the President called upon the states which were in danger to send 100,000 men to serve for six months. On the arrival of these men, one of the most terrible battles of modern times, and one that was to decide the fate of our country, was fought, lasting three days.

On July 1, the first day of the battle, the Confederates advancing, unexpectedly met the Union cavalry, commanded by General Meade, just west of Gettysburg, on the Chambersburg road.

Neither general had planned to have the fight at Gettysburg, except as a defensive one to cover up their marchings.

Reinforcements came for both sides and the Federal troops were forced back and, becoming tangled in the village streets, lost many men as prisoners.

All night long both sides were preparing themselves for the great contest which they now saw close at hand. The Union soldiers were situated on a ridge behind the rocks and ledge of a stone wall on the crest of Cemetery Ridge; while the Confederates on Seminary Ridge, about a mile and a half away, were largely hidden in the woods. Only a field of waving grain lay between the two great armies.

Next day, July 2, in the afternoon, Longstreet, the Confederate leader, led the first grand charge against General Sickles, the Union leader, who, being reinforced by General Warren, suffered no loss, but was driven back to a better and stronger position on the Ridge. Ewell, another Confederate leader, made an attack on the Federals' right and secured a good position there. This movement encouraged General Lee, who, about one o'clock the next afternoon, July 3, opened fire, with 150 guns, on the Unionists. The shells fell thick and fast for two hours. Then there was a lull and out of the woods, in double line of over a mile long, swept a magnificent column of 18,000 Confederate men, on their way to Cemetery Ridge. It was our time now, and, as the Confederate lines passed by, our guns tore great gaps in their ranks; volleys smote them everywhere; their lines broke and yet they pushed forward. On each side men admired the splendid courage of their opponents. They fought with bayonets, and even hand-to-hand;; so close were they sometimes, that the powder scorched their very clothes.

The Federals, finding they were getting the best of it, pushed on, still firing, until the Confederates could no longer stand the terrible fire, and whole companies of them rushed into the Union lines and were taken prisoners, while others fled from the field.

It was a terrible, bloody battle—the most critical of the war —for the Confederates never came so near a final success as at this time, and now, as they were defeated, and driven out of Pennsylvania, Maryland and the upper part of the Shenandoah Valley, they found that it was not so easy a matter to push the war into the North as they had anticipated. The battle was regarded as the turning point of the Civil War, and, although a great victory to the Unionists, they lost over 25,000 men, including General Reynolds; while the Confederates lost a greater number, among whom were many good officers, the like of whom—General Stonewall Jackson, Barksdale, Garnett, Armistead, Pender and Semmes—could never be replaced.

President Lincoln, on the 4th of July, issued the following despatch to the people of the North, so gratified was he at the success of our army:

"The President announces to the country that news from the Army of the Potomac, up to 10 p. m. of the 3d, is such as to cover that army with the highest honor, to promise a great success to the cause of the Union, and to claim the condolence of all for the many gallant braves fallen; and that for this he especially desires on this day, He, whose will, not ours, should ever be done, be everywhere remembered and reverenced with profoundest gratitude.

"A. LINCOLN."

It seemed strange that while this great battle was being fought another of as equal importance was raging, and that on July 3, the city of Vicksburg surrendered to General Grant all its garrison and war materials. This was a terrible blow to the Confederates, but caused the most enthusiastic rejoicings among the Unionists, and President Lincoln was serenaded, great speeches were made, and public meetings held all over the land.

On account of these victories and others, President Lincoln appointed the 6th of August as a day of national thanksgiving, and later in November another such day. During the autumn of the same year, the State of Pennsylvania purchased a part of the battlefield adjoining the cemetery for a burying place for the fallen soldiers. It was dedicated on the 19th of November, 1863, President Lincoln and Hon. E. Everett making touching and eloquent addresses.

JULY FOURTH.

Declaration of Independence.

During the Revolutionary War it was decided by the patriots that nothing now was to be hoped for from England, as their former petition to the King for redress of their wrongs had resulted in the King's Proclamation declaring the colonists in a state of rebellion. So it was decided by Congress that now was the time to renounce all allegiance to the crown.

While Congress was in session, June 7, 1776, Richard Henry Lee, of Virginia, rose and moved, "That these united colonies are, and of right ought to be, free and independent states, and that their political connection with Great Britain is, and ought to be, dissolved."

Whereupon a committee of five, consisting of Thomas Jefferson, John Adams, Benjamin Franklin, Roger Sherman and Robert R. Livingston, was appointed to draft a formal declaration of independence.

Thomas Jefferson was chosen chairman, and he, with the help of John Adams and Benjamin Franklin, drew up the Declaration, presented it to Congress, July 1, and, after three days of careful deliberation and inspection, it was amended and passed, at 2 o'clock, July 4, 1776, having been signed by John Hancock, President of Congress, and Charles Thomson, Secretary. On August 2, 1776, all members of Congress, representing the thirteen states, signed it. When a remark was passed on the largeness of John Hancock's signature, he said: "The King will be able to see that name without the aid of his glasses."

So the thirteen colonies existed no longer, but in place of

them, the grand, new United States of America. How the people, north and south, rejoiced! how they shouted! Bells rang, guns were fired and people knelt in prayer, thanking God for His goodness to them. They even tore down the leaden statue of King George III. in New York, and dragged it through the streets, thus dethroning, practically, the King in America. And afterwards, when the Americans were in need of bullets, they melted this statue and made bullets out of it, and fired them at the King's own soldiers.

Copies of the Declaration were sent to all the conventions, assemblies, and to the commanding officers of the armies to be read to their soldiers.

Old "Liberty Bell" was the first to proclaim the glad tidings over the land, and it is said that it rang "one hundred times" and, in so doing, cracked itself with joy. It is a singular fact that, when the bell was being cast, which was twenty-three years before the Declaration of Independence was signed, on it was inscribed the words: "Proclaim liberty throughout all the land unto all the inhabitants thereof."

Although cracked and voiceless now, it is the pride and glory of the people of the United States, and is safely guarded in the old Independence Hall. It was on exhibition during the World's Fair, in Chicago, Ill., 1893.

JULY TWENTY-THIRD.

Establishment of the First School in St. Paul.

In 1846, the chief of the Kaposia band went to Mr. Bruce, the Indian Agent, and asked him to establish a school, as his people wanted to reform. Mr. Bruce wrote, immediately, to Dr. Williamson, asking him to come and look over the field, which he did in November, 1846.

In order to promote education among the whites and half-breeds, he wrote to ex-Gov. Slade, President of the National Popular Educational Society, in 1847, requesting him to send Miss Harriet E. Bishop to him.

On her arrival he took her to "Pig's Eye," now known as "St. Paul," and introduced her to the citizens of the place.

So Miss Harriet E. Bishop had the honor of opening and teaching the first school in the city of St. Paul, in fact in Minnesota, excluding the mission schools, July 23, 1847. The school, or rather the blacksmith's hovel, had a bark roof, loose floor, and seats made of boards laid across pegs, driven into the walls. The visitors' seat was made of a plank, the ends of which were placed, one between the cracks of the logs, the other upon a chair. In a corner of the room was a hen's nest, and in the center a rickety old cross-legged table.

This school was situated on the corner of Third and St. Peter streets, near the site of the old brick Presbyterian Church.

On the first day of school there were but nine scholars, only two of whom were white; but when school closed, in the summer, there were thirty enrolled.

A year later the residents of Fort Snelling built a small school-house; and in November, 1848, Miss Bishop commenced her second term in a new school-house built in the upper part of the town.

In 1849 another school was built in the lower part of the town and taught by Miss Mary A. Scofield. These two schools, together with the one that the Rev. M. Hobart taught, were kept open all winter and numbered in attendance 120. The legislature, in 1849, passed laws providing, in the territory of Minnesota, for a common school system. St. Paul was the first to take advantage of the acts, and in December of the same year held meetings and established three district schools. One, at the Methodist Church on Market Street, for boys, taught by Mr. Hobart, December 10th. Another on Jackson and Fourth Streets, taught by Miss Scofield, December 24, and the third on Bench Street, in the log cabin, taught by Miss Bishop, December 24.

Laws were also passed in 1856, making St. Paul one school district, and creating a Board of Education which was to consist of nine members, elected, three from each ward.

In 1857, the first regular public school building was erected and by the end of the next year there were three public schools accommodating 606 pupils and thirteen teachers. At present there are forty-five public schools including one central high, a manual training and a teachers' training school, and a corps of nearly 500 teachers, besides eleven night schools, many private and denominational schools and colleges.

Rev. E. D. Neill, of St. Paul, was appointed the first State Superintendent of Schools, and among the city superintendents were S. S. Taylor, B. F. Wright, C. B. Gilbert and the present superintendent, A. J. Smith.

SEPTEMBER.

Labor Day.

Labor Day, a legal holiday, made for the benefit of working mankind, was first celebrated, by a few states, in 1887.

It is observed on the first Monday in September of each year, with public exercises, on labor and unions, while a part of the day is devoted to recreation.

All banks, government offices and public buildings are closed, and business is suspended.

In 1894 more than one-half of all the states in the Union made a law setting aside this day as a legal holiday.

To the Europeans is due the credit of instituting a Labor Day, they celebrating it, long ago, by demonstrations in favor of reforms, etc. It occurs on the first of May in Europe instead of in the fall of the year or September.

The State of Minnesota first observed it on September 6, 1894.

The following states and territories observe the day: Colorado, Connecticut, Iowa, Massachusetts, Nebraska, New Jersey, New York, Ohio, Pennsylvania, California, Washington (D. C.), Delaware, Georgia, Illinois, Indiana, Kansas, Maine, Michigan, Montana, New Hampshire, Oklahoma, Oregon, Minnesota, South Carolina, South Dakota, Tennessee, Texas, Utah, Virginia, Washington, Florida, Louisiana, Alabama, Idaho, New Mexico, New Hampshire, Missouri, Maryland, Rhode Island, Wisconsin and Wyoming.

SEPTEMBER NINTH.

Discovery of St. Anthony Falls.

Father Louis Hennepin, a Franciscan priest, in company with La Salle, was commissioned by the French King to explore the Mississippi Valley, trade with the Indians, and convert them to the Catholic faith.

When Father Hennepin and La Salle reached the Illinois River, La Salle turned back, while Father Hennepin, in company with a few Indians, directed his course up the Mississippi as far as Mille Lacs. On returning, in the latter part of July or August, 1680, he pitched his tent on the present site of what is now the City of Minneapolis and, on September 9, 1680, Father Hennepin gazed upon the great falls which he reverently named "St. Anthony Falls," in honor of his patron saint, "Anthony of Padua." Father Hennepin is supposed to have been the first white man to behold these falls.

The falls are about five miles above the beautiful Falls of Minnehaha, and are described as being, then, about "forty or fifty feet high, divided in the middle by a rocky island of pyramidal form, the river being narrower here than elsewhere, and the country on each side being covered with oaks and other hardwood, scattered wide apart."

It was not until eighty-six years after, or in the year 1766, that Captain J. Carver visited these falls, he being the second white man to behold them.

During the two centuries that have elapsed the Falls have greatly changed, both in appearance and position. The process of the undermining of the sand rock, which underlies the limestone, has been constantly at work; so that, in former days, these falls were probably in the vicinity of Fort Snelling. The limestone edge has been prevented from falling away, by engineering skill; what, with the hum of the mills and the working of machinery, and the crowding of commerce to-day, the picturesque charm, which once so justly celebrated the Falls of St. Anthony, has been nearly destroyed.

SEPTEMBER NINETEENTH.

Death of Garfield.

Called "The Second Martyred President."
Said: "Ideas are the great warriors of the world."

James A. Garfield, the twentieth President of the United States, was born in a log house, in the backwoods of Orange, Ohio, November 19, 1831. At the age of two years, his father died, leaving his dear mother, with four children, very poor. When four years old his devoted sister carried him to school on her back, so that he could get an education. Thomas, his sacrificing brother, did everything he could to help "Jimmy" along. At the age of twelve, Garfield helped to support the family by working at the carpenter's bench. At sixteen, we find him driving mules on a canal boat. Two years later, he enters Chester School, and at twenty-one he establishes himself as a country school teacher. In his twenty-third year he enters Williams College, where he remains, till he graduates, in 1856, aged 26. At twenty-seven, we find him principal of the Hiram Institute and a year later a member of the Ohio Senate. Three years from this, he becomes Colonel of the Forty-second regiment of Ohio, being but thirty-one years old. At thirty-two he is a Major-General, having won honor at Little Creek. On reaching his thirty-third year, he was elected a member of the Thirty-eighth Congress and, fifteen years after, a member of the United States Senate. On reaching fifty, he becomes the President of the United States.

On July 2, 1881, as he was in the railroad station of Washington, D. C., waiting the arrival of the train which was to bear him to Williams College, Massachusetts, where he was to deliver the commencement address, he was shot through the body, above the third rib, by a disappointed office-seeker, Charles J. Guiteau. This deed was done "in the most peaceful and prosperous moment that this country has known for half a century, and the shot was fired absolutely at a man without personal enemies, and a President whom even his political opponents respected."

The public was horror-stricken at the deed, and around the Christian hearth-stones family groups knelt in tearful prayers for the restoration of their noble chief. Perhaps so much united, earnest prayer for one person, ascending from even the humblest and remotest hamlet of the nation, was never before offered at the throne of grace. Doctors and surgeons were speedily summoned and the President was removed to the White House in an extremely prostrated, critical, but conscious, condition.

His first thought was about his beloved wife, who was away gaining strength after her recent illness. He sent word to her to "come home, as he had got hurt."

As the President was being tenderly lifted out of the ambulance he glanced up at the windows of the White House, raised his right hand, and gave the military salute, which seemed to say, "Long live the republic."

Garfield was very calm, hopeful and jovial during his sickness, and did not give up, although he thought his wound a very bad one, and would often say to the doctors, "Don't be afraid; tell me frankly; I am ready for the worst, and am not afraid to die."

One day, his son, James, was sobbing at his bedside: his father, looking up, said, lovingly, "Don't be alarmed, Jimmy, the upper story is all right, it is only the hull that is a little damaged."

' After the arrival of Mrs. Garfield, Mr. Garfield seemed to grow better, and the nation thought it would appoint a day for thanksgiving; but finally he grew worse and worse, and a day,

August 29, was appointed for fasting and prayer, when a whole nation bent the knee to God, beseeching Him to spare their beloved President, if it were His will. God answered their prayers for a short time, and Garfield grew better again—so much so, that his doctors thought the air of Long Branch, L. I., would be more beneficial to him than that of Washington. So the great ruler of the nation was borne carefully upon his bed to New Jersey, and along the railroad people gathered in silence, with uncovered heads and tearful eyes, to watch the train, as it moved silently by.

He was benefited by this change at first, and everybody thought he would get well, when, at thirty-five minutes past two o'clock, at night, after nine weeks of patient suffering, President Garfield died, September 19, 1881. He died as he wished, on the anniversary day of his promotion to Major General at Chickamauga.

By 12 o'clock, on the following morning, bells from Maine to California were tolling their sad tidings. Even across the water they tolled their church bells out of sympathy for us, and respect for our deceased President. Business was suspended, public buildings were elaborately draped with the emblems of mourning, and everyone mourned. Letters of condolence were sent to the nation and family from all over the world.

Garfield's remains were taken to Washington, where they were laid out in state for the thousands of sorrow-stricken people to see. The casket was covered with exquisite flowers, among them being a costly tribute, of the most elaborate floral design, from Queen Victoria.

After the impressive services, his body was conveyed to the train, which was so heavily draped in mourning that not a particle of woodwork could be seen; and thence to Ohio, his old home, for burial. Along the route, from Washington to Cleveland, the emblems of sorrow were shown. On arriving at the depot, a hearse with four black horses and four colored grooms carried the remains to the City Park, where services were held, and the people paid their last sad respects to their mortal chief. Perhaps no city in the world was ever draped so beautifully and expensively as was the City of Cleveland, Ohio. Even men, women and children wore black or a bow of crape out of respect.

The funeral procession was one of solemnity and grandeur. It was over six miles long, and the beautiful hearse, drawn by twelve beautiful black chargers, four abreast, having mourning plumes on their heads, and a black cloth fringed with silver over them, each attended by a colored groom, was a grand sight to behold.

So, amidst the magnificent and abundant floral display, the "Martyred Chief" of the land was laid to rest.

The words uttered by Garfield, on hearing of the death of Abraham Lincoln, were only too true of himself. He said: "This day will be sadly memorable so long as this nation shall endure, which, God grant, may be 'till the last syllable of recorded time,' when the volume of human history shall be sealed up and delivered to the Omnipotent Judge."

Garfield's assassin, Charles J. Guiteau, born in America, was an eccentric, weak-minded lawyer forty years of age. He had tried in vain to get an appointment as consul to some foreign country, but failed, and, being disappointed, thought that if he could get Garfield out of the way his supposed party could carry everything their own way.

He was arrested immediately after firing the shot and lodged in the District jail. He wrote a letter to General Sherman asking for protection while in jail. He received what the law allowed criminals.

He was tried November 14, 1881, convicted January 25, sentenced February 4, and hanged June 30, 1882.

He had no accomplices in the matter.

OCTOBER TWELFTH.

Discovery of America.

Columbus, the son of a poor wool-comber, was born at 27 Ponticello street, Genoa, Italy, about 1435.

At the age of fourteen, he began his sea-faring life, of which he made a success.

In 1473, he married Philippa Perestrelo and had one child, a boy, Diego.

All through his life Columbus conceived the idea that the earth was round and that by sailing westward across the Atlantic ocean he would find a nearer route to Cathay or East Indies than the route they had.

When quite old, more from disappointment than age, he asked aid of four different courts, viz., Italy, Portugal, England and Spain.

After many trials and disappointments, he finally received aid from Queen Isabella of Spain, who fitted out two small vessels with 102 men. One, the "Pinta," that saw land first, and the other "Nina, the Baby." The "Santa Maria," Columbus' flagship, was fitted out by Columbus and his friends and was the largest of the fleet.

Queen Isabella promised Columbus the title of viceroy of all the lands he discovered, one-eighth of all the precious products, and his "say" in all matters concerning his discoveries. This agreement between the Queen and Columbus was signed April 17, 1492.

Four months later, on Friday, August 3, he sailed from Palos, Spain, and landed Friday, October 12, 1492, on Guanahani, or Cat Island, now known as Watling Island. He planted the Spanish flag and knelt down and thanked God for his safe deliverance. Thinking he had reached India, he named the natives Indians and the island San Salvador, which meant "Holy Savior."

It is said that the first man to land off Columbus' fleet was an Irishman named Williams; the second, an Englishman named Law or Larkins.

Columbus remained several months on this island hunting for gold and Cathay, neither of which he found.

Through the carelessness of his cabin-boy, the Santa Maria was wrecked at Hayti, so Columbus built a fort out of what was left of it and, leaving one-half of his crew at Hayti, returned home on the Nina, taking some of the natives and products with him.

On arriving in Spain, he was received by the King and Queen with great pomp and joy, being called "Your Excellency Don Christopher Columbus. Admiral and Duke," instead of "The Crazy Explorer," as he was formerly called. Nothing seemed too good for Columbus at that time. Eevrybody loved and admired him.

There was no trouble now in getting ships or men to return with him, as everybody was anxious about the discovery of gold.

In September, 1493, with a fleet of seventeen ships and 15,000 men, Columbus started on his second expedition. His new flagship was called "Maria Galante."

He landed at Jamaica and Porto Rico the second time, and then went in search of the men he had left, and found that the Indians had killed them all and destroyed his fort. Returning to the islands, he captured some of the Indians and sent them to Spain, on the second expedition, to be sold as slaves, so as to defray some of his expenses and buy cattle for his men, who were becoming somewhat mutinous. Columbus' second expedition was a failure, and he went back to Spain sick and down-hearted, and, instead of being received with pomp and show as he was the first time, he was obliged to disguise himself as a penitent priest in order to enter the city, so powerful were his enemies, who were jealous of him. However, the King and Queen pardoned him when he related his story about his hardships and mutinous men. They fitted him out, for the third time, with six ships and men, and in the year 1498 he discovered the mouth of the Orinoco River, South America.

As there were still hard feelings among Columbus' men, Bobadilla was sent over from Spain to set matters right. On arriving, he ordered Columbus and his brother to be seized, chained and thrown in prison, Bobadilla hating them so. After a few days they were hurried off to Spain for trial and punishment. Columbus looked at his chains and said: "I shall keep them always as relics and memorials of my services."

The King and Queen ordered the chains taken off Columbus and had him released. They also sent him $5,000 and word to come and see them immediately. He did, and again asked for ships, money and men to make a fourth voyage.

After waiting for two years, he received four small caravels and 160 men. He now makes his last voyage, 1502, at the age of fifty-six years.

On his arrival in the West Indies, 1502, he was refused admittance by Bobadilla, who shortly afterwards was drowned at sea. Columbus then turned his fleet in another direction and discovered Central America, and for the first time in his life stood on the real soil of America. He named this spot Veragua, which has become the title of the family of Columbus. The Duke of Veragua, a relative of Columbus, is still living. He visited the United States in 1893, during the World's Fair.

Columbus, on finding that his vessel leaked, begged help from the Governor of Hayti. He received it, in the shape of being sent home to Spain, sick, unnoticed, unhonored and unwelcomed.

On arriving home, Columbus found the Queen dead, and he with but few friends and, although very sick, he managed to crawl to see the King, but he would do nothing for him.

So the great "Discoverer of America" gave up in despair, dying in poverty at No. 7 Columbus avenue, Valladolid, Spain, 1506, aged sixty years.

He was quietly buried and, since his first burial, his remains have been moved from one place to another, and today they are supposed to be in a leaden casket in the Cathedral of Santa Domingo, West Indies. His chains were buried with him, by request.

Over a dozen places, in the Old World and the New, have built monuments and statues in his honor. The United States, alone, has named over sixty towns and villages after him.

So the great discoverer, who thought he had reached Cathay, instead of being 5,000 miles away from it, died ignorant of the fact of his great discovery. It was his faith and persistence that discovered America, and opened a way for millions who now call it their home.

In 1893, the four hundred and first anniversary of the discovery of America was celebrated by a grand World's Fair, in the City of Chicago, Illinois.

OCTOBER NINETEENTH.

Surrender of Cornwallis.

Lord Cornwallis, commander of the British forces, fortified himself at Yorktown, a village situated on the York river, about seven miles from Chesapeake Bay, while Lafayette positioned his troops on the peninsula a few miles off and waited patiently for reinforcements from Washington, which arrived in a very short time.

Washington, the commander of the American forces, and Rochambeau, the commander of the French troops at the north, had been threatening New York, but they quietly withdrew their forces before Clinton was aware of what they were doing, and proceeded on their way to Virginia to hem Cornwallis in.

For Clinton to pursue the Americans now was useless, and Cornwallis found that he could neither get out of Yorktown, now, nor get provisions in, as the English ships that were sent to his relief were turned back by a strong French fleet that had been stationed at the entrance of the Chesapeake Bay for that purpose.

About the last of September, the British, numbering 16,000 men, took up position, and were ready for battle.

A terrible battle ensued; the outworks of the British were stormed and burned, their ships were burned near the coast, and they were repulsed at every point by the Americans. So near were the Americans' cannon to the British line that Cornwallis began to look about him for means of escape. Only one way was afforded him, and that was a cruel and hazardous one. It was to break through the French lines of 2,000 strong, first destroying all his baggage, and to leave his sick and wounded to the mercy of the enemy. Nevertheless Cornwallis tried it, but failed in the attempt, being heavily repulsed by the enemy. There was nothing left now for Cornwallis to do but to surrender, seeing his other chances were hopeless. The terms of surrender were arranged at Moore's house, which was situated on the York river near the Americans' line.

So, on the 19th of October, 1781, over 7,000 men laid down their arms in the presence of the victorious Americans. The scene was a very impressive one. The American army was drawn up in two lines over a mile long, with General Washington mounted on his noble horse, and attended by his officers and forces, on one side, with Rochambeau and his staff, at the head of the French forces, on the other side.

The British soldiers, with muskets shouldered, banners furled and sullen looks, appeared with their drums beating a British march, and marched with irregular steps slowly down between the American lines.

Lord Cornwallis did not surrender his sword himself, but sent it by General O'Hara. General Washington sent General Lincoln to receive it, because, a year or so ago, Cornwallis made General Lincoln surrender his sword to him at the Battle of Charleston.

The British soldiers were then ordered to pass into an adjoining field and commanded to lay down their arms. The redcoats were so vexed at this that many of them threw them down with such force as to break them. After this scene the prisoners were led back to Yorktown, where they were to await the orders of Congress.

Thus the proud English people lost at one blow over 7,000 men, besides all their cannon, muskets, powder, balls and provisions.

The news of this great American victory soon spread over the country like wild fire, and the joyful tidings were announced by bells ringing, cannon shooting and men shouting "Past two o'clock and Cornwallis is taken."

It is said that "an old man, the doorkeeper of Congress, dropped dead from joy on hearing the news." People went to church to give thanks, business was suspended for a time, and the names of Washington, Rochambeau and Lafayette were on the lips of everyone.

When Lord North, of England, heard the news, he acted as if he had received a cannon ball in his breast, for he thought Cornwallis could do anything.

Congress met and appointed the 13th of December, 1781, as a general thanksgiving day.

Thus the surrender of Cornwallis practically put an end to the long, tyrannical and bloody War of the Revolution.

NOVEMBER NINETEENTH.

The Establishment of the First School in Minneapolis.

Rev. J. D. Stevens, a missionary of the Presbyterian Church, taught the first school within the present limits of the City of Minneapolis in 1836. It was situated on the banks of Lake Harriet, and the pupils were native Americans, or Sioux Indians. When school first opened November 19, there were six fullblooded Indian children, none of whom could speak a word of English.

The next school taught in what is now the City of Minneapolis was a private school opened by a Miss E. Backus, June 1, 1849. It was a small frame building, or shanty, seating but twenty pupils, and was situated on Second street, near Second avenue south, St. Anthony. As the number of pupils increased so rapidly, it was found necessary to build another school, which they occupied in the winter.

The first public school was taught, for a time, by a Mr. Lee. This school was built on the East Side, by subscriptions obtained from a few of the pioneers. Among those who attended this school were Helen and Abner Godrey, Mortimer, Daniel, John and Sarah Rollins, Luella Tuttle, Emery and Elmer Worthington, and the children of Charles Mosseau and Pierre Bottineau.

The city at this time was divided into two divisions, known as the East and West divisions.

Turning to the West Division of the river, we find, on the

banks of the river near Second street and Eighth avenue south, an old governmental log building, which was used for school purposes, in 1851, by Miss Mary Schofield.

On December 3, 1852, Miss Mary E. Miller, now Mrs. M. B. Robinson, of this city, commenced school, with twelve children, in a small house on the corner of Third avenue south and Second street—the present site of the woolen factory. Miss Hartwell, now Mrs. J. D. Taylor, taught school in 1854, at the corner of Fourth street and Hennepin avenue, later at Thirtieth and Thirty-fifth streets south.

December 5th, Charles Hoag, known as the district school teacher of Minneapolis, taught school for four months in District No. 5.

In 1855, definite measures were taken to erect a public school building.

A union school was then built and opened in 1858, on the West Side, with George B. Stone as principal, and an attendance of 350 scholars.

The first rules governing the schools were then published. In the same year, the East Division was incorporated as the City of St. Anthony. Two years before, 1856, the West Division was incorporated as a town; but a city government was not organized until 1858; this was given up later. In 1867, it was again incorporated as the City of Minneapolis.

By an act of the Legislature, 1872, the cities of St. Anthony and Minneapolis were consolidated, but the school systems then in force in each division were to remain the same, under the direction of the Board of Education of the East and West Divisions of Minneapolis. When, by another act of the Legislature, approved March 7, 1878, the two school divisions were united under the one head and the Board of Directors of the West Division of Minneapolis, ceased to exist, April 1, 1878, and in place of it were elected, from the whole city, seven directors, who were to have control of all public school matters, and who were incorporated as "The Board of Education of the City of Minneapolis."

There are now fifty-six graded public schools, four high

schools and a corps of nearly 800 teachers, to say nothing of the private schools and colleges.

To show the progress of the public school system and the good work done by the Board of Education, assisted by their able superintendents, it will be well to note that in 1868, only thirty years ago, there were but twenty-seven teachers in the public schools.

Dr. Neill was appointed, by Governor Ramsey, in 1851, the first territorial superintendent of schools. Mr. A. S. Kissell, W. O. Hiskey, O. V. Tousley, John E. Bradley and Charles M. Jordan have served as city superintendents of the schools, C. M. Jordan still serving in that capacity at the present time.

NOVEMBER.

Thanksgiving Day.

A day, now appointed by the President of the United States, and then by the Governor of the State, for giving thanks to God, for his mercies to mankind through the year.

It is generally celebrated on the last Thursday in November, when the harvest is duly over.

Thanksgiving is only celebrated in those states which have provided for it by law, and the President's proclamation only makes it such for such states.

Thanksgiving had its origin among the little band of Pilgrims of Plymouth, Mass. The Puritans first celebrated it in the fall of the year 1623, when, for the first time, the harvest was seemingly abundant, and peace reigned, not only among themselves, but between the Puritans and Indians, and their dwellings were unmolested.

How the Puritan children rejoiced on this day—the first feast day in their new home—when there would be plenty of pies, cakes, puddings and wild turkey; yes, and pop-corn, too! The Pilgrims even invited strangers to their feast, the strangers being the good chief, Massasoit, and his one hundred braves, who eagerly accepted the invitation, and not only came to dinner, but early enough for breakfast, and, on departing after tea, said, in way of congratulations or thanks to the colonists, who had been so kind and hospitable to them, "The Great Spirit loves his white children best."

Thus, from this first thanksgiving, sprang the thanksgiving time all over the New England States, and at the present time has become almost a national one, being observed in all the states, though in some it is not a statutory holiday.

DECEMBER SEVENTEENTH.

Whittier's Birthday.

Called "The Quaker Poet."

John G. Whittier, the most American of all American poets, and universally recognized as the prophet poet, was born of Quaker parentage on a farm near Haverhill, Mass., December 17, 1807.

His father being a poor farmer, Greenleaf was obliged to work on the farm during the summer and attend school in the winter.

His imaginations were first aroused after reading a volume of Burns, which had been loaned to him by the country schoolmaster.

He then began to write poetry, much to the dislike of his father, who forbid him to do so.

His first poem, "The Exile's Departure," was published without Greenleaf's name, in the Garrison paper. His eldest sister sent it to the paper, he not knowing anything about it. It was received with great favor among the literary people, but no one knew it was poor little Greenleaf's work.

As his father could not afford to send Greenleaf to an academy, and as Greenleaf wanted to go very much, he learned how to make ladies' shoes and slippers, and so earned enough to send himself to Haverhill Academy for six months, after which he taught school for one year, so as to earn enough money to go the other six months. He studied for two years at the academy, and then engaged in journalism in Boston; later he became the editor of the "Haverhill Gazette." "New England

Weekly Review" and the "Pennsylvania Freeman," the office of the latter being burned by an infuriated mob, on account of its anti-slavery opinions.

He was elected to the Legislature of Massachusetts in 1835, and was secretary of the National Anti-Slavery Society. He was very strongly associated with William Lloyd Garrison in the anti-slavery movement. He wrote, up to the time of his death, for the "National Era" and "Atlantic Monthly."

He died at Hampton Falls, N. H., September 7, 1892, aged 85 years.

His poem, "Snow Bound," describing his home and a big snow storm that occurred during his childhood, was written by request. This house, that he speaks of, is still standing and is open to visitors. The things are kept in the same order as when Greenleaf lived there.

The poem, "In School Days," describes the old country school-house which he attended when a boy, and the little girl he loved. She died in girlhood and Whittier never married, so fondly attached to her was he.

Whittier loved children and pets. Among his pets were Charlie, the parrot; Friday, the squirrel; his mocking-bird, David; Robin Adair, his big shepherd dog, and Jackanapes, his little dog.

"The Barefoot Boy" is a poem written by Whittier describing his own happy country life when a boy.

He also wrote "Maud Muller," "Barbara Frietchie," and many other delightful poems.

Most of his poems savor of sympathy, honorable labor, enforced poverty, nature, humanity and Godliness.

DECEMBER TWENTY-SECOND.

Landing of the Pilgrims.

About seventy years before the Landing of the Pilgrims, the state religion of England was changed from the Roman Catholic to the Protestant; but still a large number of people were not satisfied, as there was too much form and government and not enough of the pure word of God. So many of these people wandered away from their old homes, to different parts of England, and set up local churches of their own. These people were called Separatists or Independents, and later Puritans, because they believed in the pure word of God. They still believed in the State Church, but they wanted a change in the government of the church.

This was refused them, and if they did not comply with the state rules they were punished. So, in 1608, they fled to Holland, in order to worship God as they pleased. They were now called Pilgrims, because they wandered away from their native home.

After living peaceably among the Hollanders for twelve years, they began to fear, as their children were growing up, that they would marry among the Dutch people, and, as they seemed to be a worldly class, the Pilgrims thought it best to go to a land where they could still worship God as they pleased and also save their families from the worldly follies of the Dutch.

Having heard much about America, they agreed to seek refuge there. So one day, a few men, women and children boarded the Mayflower and Speedwell and sailed for the New World. The Speedwell becoming worthless, they abandoned her, and the Mayflower, with about 102 passengers, went alone on her long and dangerous voyage, seeking a new home.

On the 22d of December, 1620, amid the winter snow and cold, this little band of Pilgrims landed at Plymouth, or on Plymouth Rock, Mass. Mary Chilton was the first woman to step foot on shore.

The Pilgrims named this spot Plymouth, after the old English town of Plymouth, it being the last place they saw when sailing away from their native land.

Before landing, Governor Carver gathered the people together in the little cabin of the Mayflower and drew up a compact in which "they agreed to enact just and equal laws which all should obey."

The storm still raged; yet, through the snow and sleet, the sturdy, true-hearted and sober-minded men commenced to build rude huts for their families.

The first winter was a severe one, and they suffered much. Everybody seemed sick or discouraged; at one time there were but seven persons well out of the whole band and, when spring came, half their little band had died; yet not one of the company thought of returning to England.

They were not troubled much with the Indians, as a pestilence had broken out in the tribe which was nearest to them, and had exterminated them.

Later on, in the spring, they were startled by a sound of "welcome," in broken English, given by Samoset, an Indian. Soon Massasoit, his chief, came and made a treaty with the Pilgrims which lasted for fifty years. Cannonicus, another chief, once sent to the Pilgrims a bundle of arrow heads wrapped in a rattlesnake's skin. Governor Bradford, the second governor, returned the skin to the Indian filled with shot and powder. Each party knew what this meant, and did not molest one another.

The Pilgrims had many trials and tribulations, yet they were thankful to God for all his favors to them.

It is said that "Elder Brewster was wont, over a meal consisting only of clams, to return thanks to God, who had given them to suck the abundance of the seas, and of the treasures hid in the sands."

Four years after the landing, the Pilgrims numbered only 184. So it was decided to assign land to each settler and let him work it himself, as the plan of working in common had failed.

From this abundance ensued and prosperity came. As the colony was never organized by a royal charter, they elected their own governors and made their own laws for seventy-two years. But in 1692, by order of the King of England, the Plymouth colony was united with the Massachusetts Bay colony and took the name of Massachusetts. Its population then numbered about 8,000, scattered throughout several towns.

The Pilgrims were a strict religious people. On Sunday morning they would all assemble, by the beat of the drum, and march three abreast, the men with their muskets over their shoulders, to the little square, wooden meeting-house, which was somewhat of a fort, too, with its six small cannon on top, to listen to a dry sermon, two or four hours long, and woe be to the one who fell asleep during the services. The women were seated on one side of the house and the men on the other.

Their laws were very rigid, and for a very small offense they were punished by ducking, whipping or by being put in the stocks, head, hands, or feet.

DECEMBER TWENTY-FIFTH.

Christmas.

The Anniversary of the birthday of our Lord and Savior, Jesus Christ.

The first certain traces of the institution of the festival of Christ's nativity to be observed are found about the time of Emperor Commodus, 180-192 A. D., although it is attributed, by the false Decretals, to Telesphorus, who flourished in the reign of Antonius Pius in 138-161 A. D.

The period of observing the nativity among the early churches does not appear with any uniformity, for some held the festival in the month of January, while others in April, or May.

Some claim that it could not be held on the 25th of December, as in Judea at that time the rainy season is at its greatest height, and shepherds could hardly be watching their flocks by night on the plains.

Again, among the causes that would fix it on the 25th of December as the proper period, and perhaps the most powerful one, is, that almost all the heathen nations regarded the winter solstice as the most important point of the year; as the beginning of the renewed life and activity of the powers of nature, and of the gods.

The Celts and Germans, from the oldest times, celebrated this season with great festivities and held their great Yule feast in commemoration of the return of the fiery sun-wheel; and many of the beliefs and usages of the old Germans, and also the Romans, relating to this matter, passed over from heathenism to Christianity. But the church sought to do away with the deep-rooted heathenish feelings and feasts, so devised the liturgy, besides the dramatic representations of the birth of Christ and the first event of his life.

So Christmas not only became the parent of many later festivals, but from it sprang the Christmas Cycle, which surpassed all other groups of Christian holidays in the manifold richness of its festal usages and furthered, more than any other, the completion of the orderly and systematic distinction of church festivals over the whole year.

So sprang the so-called "Manger Songs," and a multitude of Christmas carols, and later the Christ tree, or Christmas tree, adorned with lights and gifts, and the custom of exchanging presents, especially Christmas cards gaily illustrated with Christmas greetings.

Christmas is celebrated in different ways by d fferent people of different religions.

Within the last hundred years the festivities once appropriate to Christmas have much fallen off, as Christmas in the olden days often lasted for days and days.

Great events often fell on Christmas Day; for instance, the crowning of Charlemagne and William the Conqueror happened, the former in 800 A. D., the latter in 1060 A. D., also the conversion of the Franks took place on Christmas Day, A. D. 496.

To the Dutch we owe our Christmas visit of Santa Claus.

References.

True Story of Christopher Columbus (Brooks).
Stories of Colonial Children (Pratt).
Christmas in America (Butterworth).
Life of Washington (Irving and Johnson).
United States Histories (Montgomery's, Barnes's, Eclectic).
Annual Cyclopedia (1887).
History of Minnesota (Atwater).
Five Cent Classics.
New England Sunday.
Strange and Curious Punishments.
Father Hennepin.
From Pioneer Days to White House (Thayer).
Assassination of Lincoln (Harris).
Life of Lincoln (Coffin).
Whittier With the Children.
A Story of Garfield (Rutherford).
From Log Cabin to White House (Thayer).
Harper's School Speaker (Vols. 1 and 2).
Harper's National Fifth Reader.
Swett's Common School Selections.
Selections from Webster.
Whittier's, Bryant's, Lowell's, Longfellow's and Hemans' Poems.
Merrill's Advanced Third and Fourth Readers.
Life of Lowell (Brown and Scudder).
Notes of Whittier's Life and Friendships (Fields).
Children's Life of Lincoln (Putnam).
Description of La Salle and Hennepin.
History of Ramsey County and City of St. Paul.
History of City of Minneapolis.
Journal of Education (1887; Vol. 25).
Chambers' Cyclopedia.
Zell's Cyclopedia.
Johnson's Cyclopedia.
Life of Columbus (Irving).
Boys of '75.
Boys of '61.
Orations on Lafayette (Adams).
Clinton and Cornwallis Controversy (Earl).
Scudder's History.
Minnesota and Its Resources (Bond).

www.ingramcontent.com/pod-product-compliance
Lightning Source LLC
Chambersburg PA
CBHW020334090426
42735CB00009B/1537